## ALSO BY JOHN L. HODGE

**BOOKS:**

*Jim Crow of the Mind and the New State Laws Designed to Preserve the Idea of White Male Supremacy* (2023)

*Presidential Racism: The Words of U.S. Presidents Since the Civil War* (2020)

*Overcoming the Lie of "Race": A Personal, Philosophical, and Political Perspective* (Second Edition, 2017)

*Dialogues on God: Three Views* (2012)

*How We Are Our Enemy – And How to Stop: Our Unfinished Task of Fulfilling the Values of Democracy* (2011)

*Cultural Bases of Racism and Group Oppression: An Examination of Traditional "Western" Concepts, Values and Institutional Structures Which Support Racism, Sexism and Elitism* (co-author) (1975)

**ESSAYS IN BOOK CHAPTERS:**

"Equality: Beyond Dualism and Oppression," Chapter 6 of *Anatomy of Racism* (1990)

"Democracy and Free Speech: A Normative Theory of Society and Government," Chapter 5 of *The First Amendment Reconsidered* (1982)

**JOURNAL ARTICLE:**

"Deadlocked-Jury Mistrials, Lesser Included Offenses, and Double Jeopardy: A Proposal to Strengthen the Manifest Necessity Requirement," *Criminal Justice Journal* (Vol. 9, No. 1) (1986)

**FOR DETAILS, GO TO: JOHN L. HODGE.COM**

# The Enduring Anti-Democratic Disease Afflicting Us
# —And Its Cure

## John L. Hodge
### J.D., Ph.D.

John L. Hodge

Publisher

Published in the U.S.A,
by
John L. Hodge, Publisher
Jamaica Plain, Massachusetts
U.S.A.
Email: JLHPublisher@gmail.com



ISBN: 978-0-9831790-9-2


Printed copies available through
local and online book sellers.
For bulk orders, contact the publisher for options.

# PREFACE

Democracy in America is dying under President Donald Trump's second administration. Exercise of freedom of speech is being punished. Due process, the core of human rights, is disdained, even to the point of intentionally killing suspects without capture or trial. The right to vote is undermined so that majority choices are defeated. The right to travel has been replaced by capricious government control and high price tags. The goal of accessible healthcare for all has been abandoned, assigning those without healthcare to disease which they will spread to others. Many will die.

In short, the Trump administration is violent, cruel, and inhumane.

America is infected by an anti-democratic disease and always has been. The disease results in racism, misogyny, scapegoating, poverty, and structural deference to concentrated wealth. That disease and its cure is what this essay is about. I wrote it towards the end of the first Trump administration as Part I of a larger book, as stated in the essay. I am urgently reprinting the essay now to address the dire situation of today.

The essay in effect asks us to think more deeply about the meaning and desirability of real democracy. Real democracy is not just a political system. It is a necessary ingredient of a humane society and culture. But not only must we think more deeply, we must act quickly and decisively, without violence, if democracy in America is to be revived and expanded before it decays permanently into death. But as we act today, we also need a clear long-term picture of where we want to go, and why.

--John L. Hodge, October 1, 2025

# The Enduring Anti-Democratic Disease Afflicting Us —And Its Cure

The world is plagued with anti-democratic institutions, beliefs and behavior. These institutions, beliefs and behavior form an interactive complex that prevents real democracy from being attained.

That we call nations "democracies" in spite of these anti-democratic forces is deceptive and false. These nations are all partial democracies teetering on a wall separating progress towards real democracy on one side and tyranny or chaos on the other.

The United States is no exception. Part II of [my] book* documents the United States' ongoing legacy of white supremacy, one of the major impediments to real democracy.

Real democracy is more than a right to vote and have representatives elected by a majority. It is a way of life based on the concept of human equality. Anti-democratic forces arise from a disease that undermines equality and enables small elites to have excessive power.

As for elections, the elites decide or heavily influence what any pool of candidates will be—though their power goes far beyond elections. In the United States, these elites consist mostly of those with enormous wealth who comprise a very small percentage of the population. The general population believes that when they vote, they are freely choosing their representatives and the president, but their choices are largely determined or heavily influenced

---

* *Presidential Racism: The Words of U.S. Presidents Since the Civil War* (2020). This essay is Part I of that book.

3

without their input. Most of the people who have chosen to run for office are either wealthy themselves,[1] have the support of those who are wealthy, or obtained a prior important office or position though the support of those who are wealthy. There are exceptions, but that there are exceptions demonstrates that they are not the norm.

But the anti-democratic disease is much more than a political disease. Anti-democratic institutions pervade the entire society and include economic, educational, and religious institutions. This disease infects not only the society but also, in varying degrees, the beliefs and habits of each individual. It is within us as well as outside around us. What is within us and outside us interact and sustain each other.

The anti-democratic disease has many devastating and recognizable symptoms. Among them are beliefs and behaviors such as racism, sexism, homophobia, religious intolerance, xenophobia, tribalism, and nationalism. But the disease also generates and sustains anti-democratic institutions that support these beliefs and behaviors, just as these beliefs and behaviors support these institutions. These institutions include economic institutions — largely private corporations — that are designed to accumulate wealth to increase the wealth of a small minority, and legal structures that permit this wealth to flow into and manipulate public and political policies. These legal structures favor those with considerable wealth, because those with considerable wealth have disproportionate say in creating these structures.

Throughout human history, societies and personal relationships that have been nourished by the concept of human equality have also been infected by this anti-democratic disease. This disease has a common source, a mostly subconscious force that I call *ingrained elitism*.

What is it and what makes it a disease?

## The Foundation of Societal Health

That this anti-democratic force is a disease presupposes a concept of health. Health derives from the idea of equality that is implicit in the properly interpreted Golden Rule.[2] Broadly stated, the Golden Rule means to treat others as you would want them to treat you. This idea and its practice is the foundation of personal as well as societal health.

The Golden Rule is not some consequence of rational necessity or a commandment imposed from Above. Instead, it is a belief that seems to make sense, as many others have found. Versions of the Golden Rule have been expressed throughout history and all over the world as the core of ethical living. Its widespread acceptance is a starting point for recommending it.[3] But there is more to the Golden Rule than what it initially appears to be.

The Golden Rule presumes that you and the other have something in common in spite of observable differences. The thing in common is not visible. It is our inviolate interiority. Awareness of this interiority probably precedes recorded history. Ancient texts and inscriptions often refer to it as "soul," which is a pre-religious idea that need not be conflated with immortality or separation from the body. The other source of the Golden Rule is empathy, which also presupposes that the other has an interiority like our own.

The Golden Rule is usually hemmed in by the view that it refers only to local or bilateral personal interactions, say, of you to your neighbor. The anti-democratic disease imposes this limitation. But logically it is not so limited. It is not only the foundation for healthy personal living among your neighbors but also the foundation of a healthy, democratic society and a healthy world.

This is because the Golden Rule and the idea of human equality are necessarily connected. The idea of equality is implicit in the idea that you treat another as you would want to be treated. It means that you treat the other as equal to you, as neither inferior nor superior. But this equality is

5

not limited to you and the other, but extends also to an other not known to you but known to the other. The equality of the other known to you to the other not known to you connects your equality to the other not known to you.

To see this more clearly, begin with the assumption that you believe in the Golden Rule as applicable not only to yourself but as something others should follow. Add to this the transitive rule in mathematics. According to the transitive rule, if A=B and B=C, then A=C. If you are A and an other known to you is B, your belief in the Golden Rule establishes your equality to B, so A=B. If B knows C, your belief that others should follow the Golden Rule establishes B's equality to C, so B=C. Due to these equalities established by your belief in the Golden Rule, A=B and also B=C, and under the transitive rule, therefore, A=C. Once this triadic equality of A, B and C is acknowledged, then the equality connects indefinitely to others. If C knows D, C=D; under the transitive rule, A=D. Due to the Golden Rule, if D knows E, then D=E; under the transitive rule, A=E. And so on. Equality has no limits. You may never have met C, D, or E. They could be completely unknown to you. The transitive rule makes explicit what is implicit in your belief: that the equality that is presumed between A and B now extends to C, D, and E, and beyond without limit. Thus, your belief in the Golden Rule logically contains within it the concept of your equality to everyone, a universal equality.

The transitive rule is essential to understanding why the Golden Rule is a political, economic and social concept as well as a personal one. It logically leads to the concept of human equality, that all people are of equal humanity and worth. This concept, in turn, is the foundation of democracy, a political idea that requires that every person be enabled to have an equal voice in creating the government and society in which they live. Accordingly, this extension of the Golden Rule — the original Golden Rule extended by the transitive rule — I will call the Extended Golden Rule.

## The Extended Golden Rule[4]

The transitive rule is the logical, mathematical component that transforms a belief in the Golden Rule into the Extended Golden Rule. But the Extended Golden Rule is more than a rational concept; it opens the door to the discovery of the vitality of living. This discovery occurs, because your belief in the equality of an other opens your mind and heart to actually experiencing the equal humanity of the other. The wonderfulness of that experience, in turn, reinforces your belief in equality and encourages you to extend your belief to the equality of all others, including others whom you had not met before and others whom you will never meet but with whom you connect through empathy.[5] The Extended Golden Rule removes all barriers to empathy. The experience of the vitality of living is then freed to flow into your being.

Reinforced by these experiences, the Extended Golden Rule does not need faith or rational proof to be the ethical foundation of how you live.

Those who block these experiences with fear reinforced by their beliefs in their own greater righteousness or superiority lose out. To sustain these false beliefs, they latch onto ideologies and myths that block empathy and disable their ability to experience the equal humanity of others. Others become objects to be oppressed or disparaged and maybe killed. The anti-democratic disease, explained below, is itself rooted in a largely unconscious equality-destroying mythology.


## The Essence of Equality and the Necessity of Human Rights

But what is this equality? It does not mean that you are the same as the other. You do not look like the other. You have different relationships. You have different

7

circumstances. You are unique and different from everyone else. This means that equality is different from sameness.

The core of our equality is our inviolate interiority which everyone has yet is unique in each individual. This inviolate interiority includes everything we experience, including our emotions, feelings, thoughts and sensations. It also includes our decision-making power and the decisions that minute by minute influence what we do and our impact on the world outside of ourselves.

Thus, this inviolate interiority does not remain hidden somewhere within. It manifests itself through expression in the outer world: actions, speech, writings, art, inventions, discovery, creations, connections to others. Without these expressions, our inviolate interiority would be imprisoned, depressed and sad. Authorities often seek to deny it or suppress it, for it is a threat to them.

The expressions of one person can lead to conflict with the expressions of others. A social adjustment is needed to coordinate these expressions so that the expressions of some do not oppress the expressions of others. Our core equality is meaningless if some are enslaved, oppressed or killed by others who enjoy wealth and prosperity. Equality requires a common ground that protects us and enables our inviolate interiority to express itself in the world in a way that respects the inviolate interiority of everyone.

This common ground is implicit in and protected by the concept of human rights. Human rights are not only individual rights but also the underlying governing principles of democratic societies. Human rights, while pertaining to the individual, incorporate the social principle of *equal rights*. They are the foundation of the protection of our inviolate interiority from external abuse.

Human rights evolve over time as growing agreements about what constitutes the common core of our equality such that it deserves protection *by* government as well as protection *from* government. Laws protecting individuals from unfair discrimination are an example of protection by government. Laws protecting freedom of speech against governmental restrictions are an example of freedom from government. Regarding human rights as "natural rights" misses the point and begs the question, because "natural rights" too depend on human agreements about what constitutes the equality component of what is natural.

An international and cross-cultural agreement about these rights is the Universal Declaration of Human Rights adopted in 1948 by the United Nations General Assembly. . . . Forty-eight nations from all regions of the globe, including the United States, voted to adopt it. The purpose of these rights, as stated in its Preamble, includes affirming "the dignity and worth of the human person and in the equal rights of men and women." Without human rights, majority rule is a form of tyranny that enables any majority to oppress any minority, just as rule by an elite is tyranny over the majority. Healthy societies, thus, require human rights as their foundation. Without human rights, the idea of equality is undermined and violated.

Human rights are about societal health as well as individual health. Every society contains individuals who see flaws in the society and look for ways to improve it. They dissent from the status quo. Human rights protect dissenters from abuse by those who object to change, just as human rights equally protect everyone from dissidents if they become abusive or violent. By protecting peaceful but expressive dissenters, human rights facilitate the expression of new ideas and efforts that enable a society to progress and not stagnate.

Some propose that the ideal society is unified and harmonized with everyone playing the same pleasant tune. Those who seek to play something more interesting would be castigated. Such a society would be oppressive and devoid of the protections human rights provide to those who propose change. Often some discord is needed to jar a society out of its slumber.

Equality based in human rights is not about uniformity

9

or the suppression of individual uniqueness. It is about the dignity and worth of all human beings as unique individuals. Enforced conformity disrespects dissenters, and, thus, is contrary to human rights. A harmonized society is necessarily repressive of individual uniqueness.

The freedom of the individual is justifiably constrained whenever that freedom can be demonstrated (not merely asserted) to endanger the well-being of others. The appropriate degree of constraint is not some theoretical constant but varies with circumstances—for example, in a crowd or during a pandemic. Unfettered individualism— pure freedom—would allow individuals to suppress or deny human rights to others. As R. H. Tawney put it, "Freedom for the pike is death to the minnows."[6] Unconstrained freedom of the individual is not a societal virtue. The equality of all means that each individual respects and affirms the equal worth and humanity of every individual. This equality is the legitimate constraint on individualism, yet it is a constraint that affirms the individual as a unique being, free to voice dissent, and also equal to others.

The process whereby individuals support one another as unique and equal individuals is a social process. Individuals engaged in this process work to create and sustain a society that supports the equality and uniqueness of all individuals. This work necessarily brings them into conflict with the components of existing societies that are oppressive and support inequality.

The anti-democratic disease, which I will examine below, counteracts equality and prevents the fulfillment of human rights. None of the nations that voted for the Universal Declaration of Human Rights has yet succeeded in fully incorporating these rights into national policy. The United States, for example, has as of this writing failed to enact the proposed Equal Rights Amendment to the U.S. Constitution, which would guarantee equal rights for women. The United States, like many nations of the world,

10

also fails to fulfill Article 25 of this Declaration (among others), which states in part, "Everyone has the right to a standard of living adequate for the health and well-being of himself and of his family, including food, clothing, housing and medical care and necessary social services." In the U.S., poverty, homelessness and lack of adequate health care plague much of the society. In addition to racism, misogyny, and exclusionary immigration policies resulting from religious and racial animosities, the United States, like most countries of the world, is thoroughly infected with the anti-democratic disease, and has been since it was founded as a nation that embraced slavery and the oppression of women.


## Expressions of the Anti-Democratic Disease

Intellectual history reveals the source of presumptions that are passed on from generation to generation, usually sufficiently beneath awareness to evade scrutiny. We must delve deeply into this history to uncover the anti-democratic disease.

To find evidence of the anti-democratic disease, we have to look no further than the stated beliefs of the people historically honored as famous men. In the European and European-influenced parts of the world (including the United States and former European colonies around the world), these famous men include Plato, Aristotle, St. Augustine, Martin Luther, John Calvin, Immanuel Kant, and Sigmund Freud. They make suitable examples of the disease. Ingrained in their world-views, as well as in the views of many others who are honored, we find blatant racism, sexism, and elitism. Sexism is one of its key ingredients.

For example, Plato said, "The greatest number and variety of desires and pleasures and pains is generally to be found in children and women and slaves, and in the less

11

respectable majority of so-called free men." Aristotle said, "The male is by nature superior, and the female inferior; and the one rules, and the other is ruled; this principle, of necessity, extends to all mankind." The early Christian theologian Saint Augustine, who advocated celibacy for men to avoid the pollution of women, said, "He who is unmarried is concerned with God's claim, asking how he is to please God; whereas the married man is concerned with the world's claim, asking how he is to please his wife." The Protestant reformer Martin Luther said, "A wife ought to be obedient to her husband as her lord, be subject to him, yield to him, keep silent and agree with him as long as it is not contrary to God." Protestant reformer John Calvin said, "Wives cannot obey Christ unless they yield obedience to their husbands." The famous philosopher Immanuel Kant said that a woman's "philosophy is not to reason, but to sense." "I hardly believe that the fair sex is capable of principles." The famous psychologist Sigmund Freud said, "Women soon come into opposition to civilization and display their retarding and restraining influence. . . . The work of civilization has become increasingly the business of men, it confronts them with ever more difficult tasks and compels them to carry out instinctual sublimations of which women are little capable."[7]

The "civilization" of which Freud speaks is hierarchically structured around inequality, with men yielding power over women. Freud instructs women to "choose her husband for his paternal characteristics and . . . recognize his authority."[8] With these words, Freud expressed the views of over two thousand years of European intellectual and religious history, where men rule and are supposed to rule over women.

This "civilization" is also racist. Just as Immanuel Kant did in the late eighteenth century, Freud in the twentieth century affirmed the superiority of the European or "white" race: "Leadership of the human species" has fallen upon the "great ruling powers among the white nations."[9] Freud viewed the non-"white" peoples of the world similarly to the way he viewed women—as people not capable of controlling their instincts and who therefore should be ruled by those who can. Thus, European colonialism is viewed not as the brutal, exploitative system that it was but as the proper order of things.

Ironically, Freud had to escape from the Nazis even though they shared a common view of civilization as consisting of the inferiority of women and the superiority of a so-called "white race" of which Freud saw himself as a member. This view of civilization is thoroughly ingrained in our culture, as indicated by the continued honoring of these famous men throughout much of the educational system.[10]

The inequality of men and women and the view of the superiority of men was openly advocated by these honored men, and, in addition, Immanuel Kant and Sigmund Freud openly advocated European or "white" supremacy. While apologists try to separate out the flaws in these honored thinkers from the rest of their views, they are blind to the idea that these flaws are a part of an overall framework of hierarchical thinking that assumed the inequality of people and the innate superiority of some over others. There was no room for democracy in their schemes. To honor them (as opposed to studying them due to their influence) and to advocate for democracy is a contradiction.


## The Anti-Democratic Disease: Ingrained Elitism

These honored men expressed the view that society should consist of hierarchical inequality. Men are viewed as superior to women. The so-called "white race" is viewed as superior to others. This superiority is not just conceptual. It is assumed that this superiority entitles the superior to rule the inferior. It is the formula supporting unequal societies governed by ingrained elites. This way of thinking is the

13

anti-democratic disease.

An essential feature of this diseased way of thinking is that the major components of the hierarchy are ingrained — that is, either unchangeable or changeable only with significant difficulty. One's position in the hierarchy is largely determined by factors over which individuals have little or no control. Whether you were observed at birth as male or female cannot be changed. Though some become transgendered, any transition made later is difficult and attempted only by a relative few. Similarly, whether you are classified as "white" at birth or not "white" cannot be changed. Though some who are initially classified as not "white" are able to change that classification later, they are able to do so only if they have a certain appearance, and relatively few take the additional effort to do so. Those born with wealth are likely to stay wealthy; those born in poverty are likely to stay in poverty, and the exceptions do not alter these likelihoods. The hierarchy is either determined or largely determined. As Aristotle stated in his advocacy of hierarchy, "For that some should rule and others be ruled is a thing not only necessary, but expedient; from the hour of their birth, some are marked out for subjection, others for rule."[11]

The hierarchical structure of society is, in turn, a component of a larger view of the entire universe as a mostly or completely pre-determined hierarchical distribution of beings. This view of the universe was exposed by Arthur O. Lovejoy in his book, *The Great Chain of Being*.[12] The Great Chain of Being "was the conception of the plan and structure of the world which, through the Middle Ages and down to the late eighteenth century, many philosophers, most men of science, and, indeed, most educated men, were to accept without question – the conception of the universe as a 'Great Chain of Being,' composed of an immense, or . . . of an infinite, number of links ranging in hierarchical order from the meagerest kind of existents . . . to the highest possible kind of creature."[13]

14

Lovejoy, however, could perceptively see the past but did not see how embedded this hierarchical conception remains in present-day culture.

In addition, Lovejoy did not draw out the full political relevance of the Great Chain of Being as being not simply a metaphysical or theological ranking but a justification for a hierarchical distribution of power that entitles those higher in the order to rule over those who are lower. Accompanying the belief in the hierarchical order of the universe was the idea that those lower in the hierarchy exist to serve those higher. After all, why else would God create the lower beings? Implicit in this idea of service is the idea that those higher in the hierarchy have a right and even a duty to compel such service. Thus, service by those lower translates into power over the lower by those who are higher. The hierarchical distribution of power is a chain of command. The Great Chain of Being is a political tool favoring those in power whereby those at the top have the greatest power and those at the bottom are the subjects of those above, where the purpose of those who are lower is to serve those who are higher. Political authority and theological authority thus unite in perpetuating a concept that supports the power of some over others.

This implicit chain of command is why this paradigm of the universe requires social and political hierarchies. In tracing practices that led to the acceptance of slavery in the land that became the United States, historian Betty Wood described sixteenth and early seventeenth century England as "characterized by a strong sense of hierarchy." "The Great Chain of Being provided theoretical support for the proposition that social rank was predetermined and unalterable, that some were born to be gentlemen and to govern while others, the majority, were fated to be poor and to provide labor, and this was the actuality of life. . . ."[14] The idea translated into the structuring of daily life. The slavery that emerged subsequently in America fit neatly into this hierarchical scheme and fortified the racism that continued after slavery and plagues America and much of the world today.

Although the Great Chain of Being may seem to be nothing more than an abstract ancient idea with little practical relevance today, instead it is thoroughly embedded in our current way of life. The distinction between mind and body becomes mind over body; the mind should rule. The distinction between reason and emotion becomes reason over emotion; reason should dominate over emotion. The difference between male and female becomes male (or to some, female) superiority. Differences of skin color mean that one is better than the other. Differences among nations and cultures mean that some are superior to others and that the superior should dominate the others and coerce them into service. The rich are seen as superior to the poor and should have more power. In all facets of our lives we seek out and honor who is best and ignore or belittle the necessary contributions of others who are under-appreciated. The educational system typically ranks students through a grading system and demeans those towards the bottom. Revolutionaries may seek to turn the vertical hierarchy upside down, creating another hierarchy with themselves at the top, while ignoring the notion of a mostly horizontal society with some flexible rounded hills and gentle slopes. The presumption of hierarchy means that we are generally inclined to see most things dualistically as either above or below other things, and thus separated from one another, and are less inclined to see different things as together side by side. Our default way of thinking is that of separateness, "either/or," not of togetherness, "both/and."[15] The Great Chain of Being is the underlying premise that is everywhere so we do not see it. But we must see it to address its pervasive influence.

Lovejoy traces the idea of The Great Chain of Being back 2400 years to Plato and Aristotle, the two men still regarded today in academia as the primary philosophers at the root of "Western" civilization. But these philosophers also fed the roots of sexism, racism and elitism, also prominent features of "Western" civilization (and elsewhere). Plato's hierarchy placed rationality at the top, emotions at the bottom. This set the stage for the culturally ingrained dualism of mind and body, reason and emotion. His pupil Aristotle said, "For that which can foresee by the exercise of mind is by nature intended to be lord and master, and that which can with its body give effect to such foresight is a subject, and by nature a slave."[16] Thus, he asserts social hierarchy as necessary, with physical laborers at the bottom. His predecessor, Plato, set forth the concept of social hierarchy in *The Republic*, wherein he asserts with his Divided Line that society must be ruled by an intellectual elite, philosopher-kings, for the majority of humankind are governed by passion and emotion, which is unsuitable for governing.

These views underlie modern societies. Physical laborers, identified with the body, are paid less, even though their work is as essential to the functioning of society as corporate executives, identified with the mind, who get paid hundreds or thousands times more. Women and people identified as "black" are viewed as more emotional than men and people identified as "white" are seen disproportionately as the holders of reason. The idea of reason over emotion prevails.[17] Accordingly, our society is Aristotelian at its core.

Freud incorporated this hierarchy of reason over emotion into the human psyche, postulating an id as the holder of passion and emotion that must be controlled by developed superegos. He identified the rational superego with the European male who has the task of maintaining control over the id of women and non-Europeans. This hierarchy, to him, is the very foundation of civilization.[18]

The fallacy of this hierarchy of reason over emotion was succinctly exposed by Jose Ortega y Gasset: "A moral system which is geometrically perfect but leaves us cold and is no spur to action is subjectively immoral. The ethical ideal

17

cannot content itself with being the most correct of ideals: it must also succeed in arousing our emotions."[19] Instead of this emotionless Platonic ideal form of truth and the good, mind and body, reason and emotion, superego and id must function together on the same level as equal partners.

Social hierarchy, thus, is not just something that happens through exercise of might but is seen as something that ought to happen, with an ingrained elite as rulers or administrators. Throughout history this kind of hierarchy has been assumed to be the ideal of social order. This assumption is reflected today in our social structure and institutions and penetrates throughout our culture, as further explained below. The ideal of hierarchy is a pervasive ideology, ingrained in our mostly unconscious way of thinking, connecting the ancient past to the present and standing in the way of progress towards a more humane future.

**Ingrained Hierarchy Today--Wealthocracy**

Against this history of the ideal of ingrained hierarchical social order has emerged the idea of democracy based on the idea of human equality. Ingrained hierarchy, which incorporates ingrained elitism, and human equality are necessarily in conflict.

The conflict was apparent from the beginning of the founding of the United States. The 1776 American Declaration of Independence courageously announced the idea of human equality, and several paragraphs later spoke of "the merciless Indian savages." The celebrated American Revolution was fought and won, because the North joined with the South when the South's purpose for entering the war was to preserve slavery and protect itself from the English court decision, *Somerset* v. *Stewart*,[20] which had effectively ended slavery in England four years before the signing of the Declaration.[21] The July 4th celebrations are, in effect, a celebration of continued slavery. The power of the South continued after the Revolution. The U.S. Constitution provided that certain people not regarded as "white" be counted as three-fifth of a person for the purpose of determining representation in the House of Representatives,[22] giving the South greater per-capita representation of free people than in the North. Furthermore, slavery was permitted by the U.S. Constitution, and after the Constitution was ratified, slavery continued for over seven decades until the Civil War. Slaves were defined by the laws of many southern states not as people but as property. Thus, they were not three-fifths of a person except for counting purposes; they were zero-fifths of a person for all other purposes. After slavery ended, many states, particularly in the South, enacted laws that separated "whites" from non-"whites." These apartheid laws (called "Jim Crow" and "segregation") were not fully abolished until 1967 when the U.S. Supreme Court decided that states cannot prohibit "interracial" marriages.[23]

The U.S. Constitution, when it became effective in 1789, contradicted the idea of human equality, revealing the strength of the enduring anti-democratic disease and its source, the Great Chain of Being. Remarkably, and widely misunderstood today, the U.S. Constitution did not grant to anyone the right to vote and still does not require universal suffrage.[24] The right to vote was left to the states, and the states then confined this right to an ingrained elite of property-owning "white" males until some states later broadened the franchise. The 15th Amendment (1870) to the Constitution, worded negatively, does not create a right to vote but only says that whatever right to vote that might exist cannot be denied "on account of race, color, or previous condition of servitude." Members of the U.S. Senate were not elected by popular vote until 1913 with the ratification of the 17th Amendment — but at that time women could be excluded from any right to vote. The right to vote contained in state laws was permitted to be confined to males until 1920 with the enactment of the 19th Amendment. Today, the popular vote still does not elect the President. That task is assigned to electors who are chosen under various state laws. Presidents George W. Bush and Donald Trump [in 2016] both lost the national popular vote and were selected by electors.

As Alexander Keyssar documented, "The principle of 'one person, one vote' — and its underlying presumption that the votes of all individuals should count equally — does not yet apply to presidential elections. . . . According to the Supreme Court . . . presidential electors [ ] need not be chosen by popular vote at all."[25] The conservative judicial ideology maintaining that the constitutionality of a law depends on what the framers intended is itself a product of the anti-democratic disease, *for the framers of the U.S. Constitution did not create or intend to create a democracy.*

The consequences of the non-democratic and even anti-democratic U.S. Constitution are apparent today. Police patrol many "black" neighborhoods as an occupation force and brutalize or kill their occupants without being convicted of assault or murder. Protestors and news reporters are shot and injured with rubber bullets, with the implicit threat that the next time the rubber may be replaced with lead. People who live in the United States today who are not U.S. citizens are, in varying degrees depending on their status, denied fundamental human rights. People who are considered to be present illegally have none of the human rights protections that should be accorded to all people. They have been imprisoned and often deported without the due process of law that citizens are entitled to. Migrants seeking to enter the United States from Mexico have been incarcerated by U.S. agents under inhumane and brutal conditions; young children have been taken from their parents. These are gross violations of human rights, but no international court has assumed the power to convict the United States of its crimes against humanity.

In the United States, the political power yielded by the extremely wealthy contrasts sharply with the subservient position of the poor. Although it is possible for a poor or middle-class person to become wealthy, and some do, overall the wealthy are an ingrained elite where wealth is passed on to their children. Rising out of poverty is very difficult and possible only for a tiny few. Many accept the idea that the poor deserve to be poor and should not be given any benefits that might help them emerge from poverty. Many would even deny them health care.

This power yielded by the wealthy, however, is not an anomaly. Instead, it is what the framers of the Constitution intended. This country was founded on the belief that the propertyless should have little or no say in what the government is or does. Today it follows from that belief that those with the most wealth should have the most say.

While the framers wisely created a barrier between religion and government, they did not and did not intend to create a barrier protecting government from concentrated wealth. Such protection could begin with protecting the electoral process from the influence of concentrated wealth, for this process depends on campaign contributions that largely determine who the elected officials will be. Such a protection must be created if real democracy is to be attained.

Building a barrier that protects government from religion was relatively simple and accomplished within a single sentence of the First Amendment that prevents Congress from passing any law respecting any religion. Preventing concentrated wealth from influencing campaigns for elected government office is more difficult and requires creative legislation developed over time involving trial and error. Congress and many state legislatures were engaged in making such legislation, but the U.S. Supreme Court effectively blocked these efforts by declaring that expenditures for political campaigns was a form of free speech protected by the First Amendment, and further declared that corporations could also "speak" with money.[26] In some respects this seems ludicrous, but, on the other hand, the U.S. Supreme Court logically continued what the framers created, a legal framework where wealth in the form of property, including shares of corporations, provides its owners with rights and privileges that others should not have, including the right to influence and determine the makeup of the government.[27]

Thus a constitutional amendment will be needed to override the Supreme Court's decision and enable federal and state legislatures to find ways to create legal barriers preventing concentrated wealth from dominating the electoral process and thereby shaping the government. Such an amendment might read like this: "The legislative power of Congress and of each state shall include the power to make laws that regulate direct or indirect expenditures for any political campaign for any state or federal office, including expenditures by candidates supporting their own campaigns, and may provide for exclusive public sources of campaign financing, provided that such expenditures or financing are sufficient to insure reasonable and fair public exposure for all candidates." [28]

In spite of the daring, historic words that introduced the Declaration, the anti-democratic disease infected everything that followed, even in the Declaration itself. What the U.S. Constitution created was not a democracy but a wealthocracy, a society in which the wealthy have the greatest influence and get the greatest benefit. The Constitution will have to be amended to remove its own impediment to real democracy. This will be difficult to achieve but necessary if real democracy is to be attained, even though by itself such an amendment will not end racism and sexism—which must end.

## Democratic and Anti-Democratic Hierarchies

There are three essential kinds of hierarchies of relevance here.

- Ingrained hierarchies of power, where those at the top are an ingrained elite who have power over those below;
- Hierarchies of simple ranking which do not involve power or lead to power later;
- Democratic hierarchies which involve the granting of power that is temporary and not ingrained.

The absence of any hierarchy is not a sensible option for society or personal living. Hierarchies of simple ranking, which do not involve power, are necessary and useful guides. When you make a grocery list and state first and second choices in case the first choice is not available or too expensive, you are creating a hierarchy of ranking. In sports, players are ranked and compete as part of the game. As long as a player at the top has no power to win aside from skill at playing the game, ranking is part of the fun of the sport and has no political implications. Hierarchies of ranking are not always harmless, however, as many such hierarchies are intertwined with ingrained hierarchies of power.

Hierarchies of power go beyond simple ranking and involve the power of those above over those below. But unlike ingrained hierarchies of power, in democratic hierarchies power is temporary and subject to continual redistribution. To accomplish specific tasks, hierarchies are useful when leaders are chosen to help guide and coordinate others, or when representatives are chosen to express what others want. Such hierarchies are necessary to minimize chaos and to enable effective action. In democratic hierarchies, however, the power of leaders is granted to them temporarily by those who have chosen to be led.

Those who have chosen to be led retain the power to change the leaders, and no power is granted to the leaders that could enable them to maintain themselves in positions of leadership. If a leader seeks to use the position of leadership to remain as leader contrary to the desires of those led, the leader has become corrupt and must be removed.

Ingrained hierarchies are ingrained largely because they are hierarchies of power that give those with power the ability to maintain themselves in control. Democratic hierarchies are transient, subject to the desire of those who are led, whereas ingrained hierarchies continue with minimal regard to those who are led. Democratic hierarchies embody the idea of human equality. Ingrained hierarchies assume and perpetuate inequality.

Corporations are typically controlled by shareholders in proportion to the number of shares they own, making them hierarchies of power based on wealth. The largest shareholders of large corporations are generally members of the ingrained elite, a few of whom have joined recently and will remain due to their enormous wealth.

The goal of creating real democracies, thus, includes the goal of replacing ingrained hierarchies with democratic hierarchies or regulating ingrained hierarchies to serve the public.

## How These Historical Forces Divide Us

The contradiction between the idea of democracy based on human equality and the idea of a hierarchical society ruled by ingrained elites is played out today in countries that are called "democracies." The United States is not an exception but a prime example of this contradiction.

One expression of this contradiction is the visible division of the United States into two Americas. One commentator, John Blake, summed up the conflict: "These two Americas have long co-existed. One is the country represented by the Statue of Liberty, and its invitation to poor and tired immigrants 'yearning to breathe free.' The other is the one that virtually wiped out Native Americans, enslaved Africans, excluded Chinese immigrants in the late 19th century and put Japanese Americans in concentration camps."[29]

Along the same line, another commentator, Robert Kuttner, sees America as consisting of "two deeply antagonistic cultures each convinced that the other is ruinous."[30] He likens the conflict to a civil war potentially headed towards a violent one—although the violence is already occurring with mass shootings by civilians, killings by police, vehicle and other attacks on protesters, rubber bullets shot at news reporters and photographers, and intimidation by heavily armed right-wing extremists, all of which have become increasingly a part of the background of daily life.

The violence is disproportionately aimed at non-"whites" and their supporters. Kuttner plausibly states, "The central driver [of civil conflict] is America's founding stain—deep, persistent, brutal racism."[31] Racism, for example, is an undercurrent in the U.S. Supreme Court's creative interpretation of the Second Amendment[32] that gives individuals the right to own weapons to protect themselves against criminals (viewed generally as disproportionately "black") and perhaps too against a government that may someday be controlled by today's minorities who together are predicted to become a majority in a few decades.

But if we look beyond the racism, we will see that the newly interpreted Second Amendment also favors the wealthy, for it allows the wealthy to own and distribute the most sophisticated and largest quantity of weaponry against which a poor man with his treasured rifle has no chance. Weapons are not just for defense, they are also for offense, and heavily armed right-wing militia are an offensive threat to any progress the United States may take towards greater equality. This threat helps preserve the status quo.

But while the conflict between the ingrained elite and those who seek the realization of human equality play out visibly in societal-wide conflict, the long-term threat to democracy is not only this visible conflict but also the heretofore hidden conflict between unconscious acceptance of ingrained elitism and the goal of realizing the idea of human equality. This conflict is not only the externally visible one but also one that has existed hidden throughout the culture and within every brain. It is not simply a conflict with the presently existing ingrained elite but with the societal acceptance of *any* ingrained elite.

The presently existing ingrained elite is also divided, as many of them are not happy with those who today control or stifle the government. It may be necessary strategically to support the efforts of some members of the ingrained elite in order to depose a current ingrained elite to make it possible for the United States to move forward instead of stagnating or disintegrating into greater violence or chaos. But, if we are to favor human equality, we must not look to some component of the ingrained elite for salvation but see that ingrained elitism itself is what must be increasingly dismantled.

Thus, the existence of two conflicting Americas is both a product of the historical conflict between ingrained elitism and human equality and a distraction from the long-term goal of eliminating ingrained elitism altogether.

## What Real Democracy Would Mean

Real democracy — not the societies of today that we call "democracies" — is the social and political setting that incorporates the Extended Golden Rule into daily life. Real democracy requires, among other things, that each person has sufficient resources and opportunity to live a life that is fulfilling. According to an astute observer of Nordic culture and politics, Anu Partanen, government should "make sure that citizens, all citizens, have equal opportunities for well-being—to pursue happiness, enjoy freedom, and achieve success."[33] This cannot be achieved if some people live in poverty. As long as there is poverty relative to the rest of the population, real democracy has not been achieved.

Real democracy would also require the elimination of racism, sexism and all forms of discrimination against defined groups. It would require equal access for all in choosing their representatives to governing bodies without any advantages given to those with greater wealth. The electoral process would be protected from concentrated corporate and personal wealth.

No nation has yet attained real democracy. Attaining it is a work in progress. It has not been attained, because the Great Chain of Being is a barrier. It will remain a barrier unless we rethink the role of hierarchy in our society, in our culture, and in our personal lives, and alter the role of hierarchies to make them compatible with democracy.

Real democracy also requires recognizing that human equality extends to those who do not believe in human equality. Without this recognition, we would engage in a contradiction that divides the world into those who are equal because they believe in human equality and those who are lesser beings because they do not believe in it. That contradiction would be a denial of human equality in the name of human equality, the same as denial of democracy in the name of democracy.

An example of the absurdity of imposing democracy by force occurred when the United States invaded Iraq in 2003 which then-president George W. Bush ordered—with the initial overwhelming support of the public[34]—to bring "freedom" to that country. The loss of hundreds of thousands of Iraqi lives was mostly ignored in America, since it was widely assumed that only American deaths were worth counting. This invasion to expand democracy

27

regarded Iraqis not as equal people but as essentially irrelevant in the global scheme of things. While maintaining a democracy means protecting it against forces that would destroy it if they are not contained, it cannot mean expanding democracy through war and violence.

President Bush's egregious error, and the error of the public that initially supported him, resulted in a military, economic and humanitarian disaster, but the antecedent error was mental. The anti-democratic disease—ingrained elitism—is a way of thinking, an unconscious ideology that is a force that opposes the idea of human equality. In the Great Chain of Being, Iraqis were not placed as highly as Americans. To combat ingrained elitism, we must recognize its presence and its effect on our social, political and economic structures. If we do not, real democracy will never be fully realized and existing societies called democracies may disintegrate into authoritarian rule or chaos.

But although this disease is a way of thinking, we must not make the mistake of calling this disease *merely* mental. The disease kills people. It supports the lack of community control over police forces, whose members are often allowed to kill and use brutal force disproportionally against ethnic minorities and those who protest these allowances. It underlies the advocacy of war, the sexist treatment of women by men, the racist treatment of people with darker skins, immigration policies based on color and religion, the hierarchical structure of corporations that enables wealth to create more wealth without regard to the welfare of all, the creation and allowance of poverty, the permission given to the wealthy to have greater influence over government and politics, and the policies of the government so influenced that disproportionately benefit the wealthy and, in varying degrees, impoverish the remainder.

The stable existence of these structures with their ingrained elites in turn reinforce mental assumptions that such hierarchy is natural, that some people deserve more power than others. Since the society is structured to give some people more power than others, it can easily be assumed that what is, is what should be. Inequality is embedded in the structure of nearly every facet of life. These structures must be altered to enable the idea of human equality to be fulfilled.


## Many Small Steps Required to Move Forward

Usually social change requires many steps, not a sudden leap from the present to the desired future. The United States Constitution, for example, has moved from its undemocratic and pro-slavery beginnings towards a greater degree of democracy through the process of many amendments over many decades. In addition to these amendments, Congressional legislation has been needed to fill in the gaps: the Civil Rights Act of 1964, for example. More amendments and more legislation, local and national, will be needed to continue this progress.

Needed change has also occurred in the form of governmental regulation of the economy, which has grown step by step over many decades. As a result, any imagined line between capitalism and socialism has been blurred. The idea that extensive governmental regulation is necessary for the economy to work is now deeply rooted.

It is, thus, important to give credit to steps in the right direction even though there are many steps left to take. Small steps should not be belittled as not being the whole step, for successful social change generally requires many small, achievable incremental steps, not one gigantic one that rarely happens or, when it does, results in another oppressive hierarchy. There is not one right path to change, but many paths to take and explore.

Some steps, however, are essential if ingrained elitism is to be overcome. One essential step is to transform the role of police. Finding a solution to doing this is simple: Do what

Camden, New Jersey did in 2013 and subsequently.[35] Continued widespread failure to do this or something similar is an unfortunate testament to the enduring strength of the anti-democratic disease.

Altering hierarchical structures also includes transformation of the structure and purpose of corporations, now owned mostly by the wealthy that exist for the openly expressed primary purpose of creating more wealth. Many European nations have taken a small but progressive step by adopting a policy of co-determination ("Mitbestimmung") that requires workers to be represented on corporate boards (currently illegal in the United States).[36] The long-term goal, however, is to regulate corporations so that their effective purpose is to benefit society as a whole and not just a wealthy elite.

Another example of a partial step in the right direction is in the parts of the sports world that place a cap on teams' wealth or use of wealth, in order to further fairness. Some major sports leagues impose limits on how much each team can spend on its players' salaries. Teams that go over this limit face heavy fines. This places a limit on the ability of a wealthy team to buy the best players and remain dominant. Instead, a team that wins the championship one year may have to shed some of its most expensive players to avoid the fine. Some of the expensive players may have to be redistributed, giving other teams a better chance to enter the top tier and compete for a championship. The team that is the champion one year may come in last the next year. Elite teams are less likely to become ingrained over long periods of time. Transient elitism and hierarchically ranked teams and players are a legitimate and necessary part of sports, but, through league rules that place a cap on team wealth or control its use, *ingrained* elitism is countered and reduced. It is not a perfect process, but it is based on a sound idea and a step in the right direction.

The economy as a whole could work similarly to this part of the sports world by imposing heavy taxes on individual and corporate wealth that exceed a reasonably high threshold. The money collected from the tax could be used to fund benefits for the rest of the population. This would be a partial remedy to the effects of wealth inequality.

Advancing towards real democracy will require additional amending of the United States Constitution to further separate it from its original anti-democratic formulation. The next steps need to be the ratification of the proposed Equal Rights Amendment and the direct election of the president by popular vote without the intervention of the Electoral College. The longer-term goal, and the most essential one, is an amendment that would protect the electoral process from concentrated wealth.

Overall, we must change the existing structures that preserve an ingrained elite, but so that they are not replaced by different structures that are equally anti-democratic.


## And a Big Step towards Curing the Anti-Democratic Disease

The anti-democratic disease is a mental and ethical pandemic that infects the world—inside us as well as outside us—and has infected it throughout human history. The vaccine that could protect us from and cure us of this disease is the Extended Golden Rule, as explained above.

The power of the Extended Golden Rule begins with recognition of our inviolate interiority and the realization that others have it too. When this recognition is combined with empathy, we establish the means of emotionally connecting to others. The Golden Rule is the ethical guide for relating to others in a way that is fruitful and respectful. It implicitly contains the idea of our equality to others. But the Golden Rule as traditionally viewed has been limited to our actual interactions with others, and sometimes limited further to bilateral relationships. The transitive rule frees it from these constraints and generates the idea of universal

31

human equality. Human rights enters the picture as the societal and governmental way of coordinating our individualities with others so that the idea of universal equality can be realized in daily life while our individualities are preserved.

While human rights are essential for the protection of this individuality, there are cultural influences lurking in every corner that can get in the way of equality. One critical example of these influences is the tendency of groups to take on a reality of their own that often subordinates the group members to a group identity. This subordination occurs whether group identity is imposed on others by those who assume their own group identity, or is imposed on themselves by members of the group. When this subordination occurs, the members of the group are not viewed primarily as individuals but primarily as components of the group. This is typical of cults, but this practice is much more widespread. The separation of people's identities into "racial," ethnic, national, class, or religious groups provides examples that pervade the entire society.

Although all group identities do not have to function this way, often group identities are locked inside mental gates that encourage the confinement of empathy to within the group and disparage its extension beyond the group. When these identities function this way, they are denials of human equality beyond the group.

Instead of locked gates, the universal equality generated by the Extended Golden Rule unlocks the gates that disconnect us from others, opening us to experiencing others in an empathetic and loving way that inexplicably enhances the enjoyment and meaning of life. These experiences are a fountain of vital energy that injects passion and emotion into the rational formula of equality. This vital energy is not only personally fulfilling, it is also needed to defeat the disease that has prevented real democracy from occurring and to make the societal-wide

32

and cultural changes needed to embody the idea and practice of human equality.

John L. Hodge
July 15, 2020

## NOTES

1. In 2018, fifty-two United States Senators (52%) each had a net worth of one million dollars or more and an average per senator net worth of over nine million dollars. https://www.rollcall.com/wealth-of-congress/ . In contrast, in 2016 the bottom 50% of U.S. families had a median net worth of $40,000, and the bottom 25% had a median net worth of $200. The *mean* net worth of the bottom 25% was negative. *Federal Reserve Bulletin*, Sept., 2017 (Vol. 103, No. 3), p. 13; https://www.federalreserve.gov/publications/files/scf17.pdf .

2. The incorrect interpretations and objections of Immanuel Kant and Herman Melville are refuted in my book, *How We Are Our Enemy – And How to Stop: Our Unfinished Task of Fulfilling the Values of Democracy* (Jamaica Plain, Mass.: John L. Hodge, Publisher, 2011), pp. 142 – 147.

3. See Jeffrey Wattles, *The Golden Rule* (New York and Oxford: Oxford Univ. Press, 1996).

4. I previously called this "the golden guide" in *How We Are our Enemy – And How to Stop*, pp.147 ff.

5. The relevance of empathy is nicely portrayed in Lynn Hunt, *Inventing Human Rights* (New York: W.W. Norton, 2007).

6. *Equality* (London: George Allen & Unwin, 1964), p. 164 (first published in 1931).

7. Plato, *The Republic*, trans. D. Lee, 2nd ed. (Baltimore: Penguin Books, 1974), p. 202. Aristotle, *Politics*, 1254b, in *The Basic Works of Aristotle*, ed. R. McKeon (New York: Random House, 1941) pp. 1132. St. Augustine, *Confessions*, Bk. II, #2, trans. R. S. Pine-Coffin (Baltimore: Penguin, 1961), p. 44. Martin Luther, "Treatise on Good Works," trans. W. A. Lambert, revised by J. Atkinson, *Luther's Works*, v. 44 (Philadelphia: Fortress, 1966), p. 98. John Calvin, *The Epistle to the Ephesians*, 5:22; contained in *Calvin's Commentaries: The Epistles of Paul the Apostle to the Galatians, Ephesians, Philippians and Colossians*, trans. T. H. L. Parker (London: Oliver & Boyd, 1965). Immanuel Kant, *Observations on the Feeling of the Beautiful and Sublime*, trans. J. T. Goldthwait (Berkeley, CA: Univ. of California Press, 1960), pp. 79, 81. Sigmund Freud, *Civilization and Its Discontents*, trans. James Strachey (New York: W. W. Norton, 1962), pp. 50-51.

8. *An Outline of Psycho-Analysis*, trans. James Strachey (New York: W. W. Norton, 1949), p. 51.

9. "Reflections upon War and Death," trans. E. Colburn Mayne, in *Character and Culture*, ed. Paul Rieff (New York: Collier Books, 1963), p. 108; also see p. 113. See Freud, *Totem and Taboo* (New York: W. W. Norton, 1950), pp. 2, 3 n.2, 12 ff, 40-41, 54 & 139. See Immanuel Kant, *Education*, trans. A. Churton (Ann Arbor: Ann Arbor Paperbacks, 1960), p. 4.

10. A thorough examination of the views of Plato, St. Augustine, Luther, Calvin, and Freud is contained in John L. Hodge, D. K. Struckmann & L. D. Trost, *Cultural Bases of Racism and Group Oppression* (Berkeley, CA: Two Riders Press, 1975), pp. 97ff and 123ff. A condensed version of this examination that added Immanuel Kant is contained in John L. Hodge, *How We Are Our Enemy – And How to Stop*, pp. 42 ff.

11. *Politics*, 1254b; contained in *The Basic Works of Aristotle*, ed. Richard McKeon (New York: Random House, 1941), p. 1132.

12. (New York: Harper & Bros., 1960) (originally published in 1936).

13. *Ibid*, p. 59.

14. Betty Wood, *The Origins of American Slavery* (New York: Hill and Wang, 1997), p. 13.

15. I described this as a feature of Dualist culture in *Cultural Bases of Racism and Group Oppression*, Part VI.

16. *Politics*, 1252a; contained in *The Basic Works of Aristotle*, ed. Richard McKeon (New York: Random House, 1941), p. 1128.

17. This is thoroughly analyzed in Hodge, et al., *Cultural Bases of Racism and Group Oppression*.

18. See Freud, *Civilization and its Discontents* and the analysis of Freud's views in Hodge, et al., *Cultural Bases of Racism and Group Oppression*, Part IV, Section 5.

19. *The Modern Theme*, trans. J. Cleugh (New York: Harper Torchbooks, 1961), p. 48 (originally published in 1923 as *Tema de nuestro tiempo*).

20. 98 ER 499; 12 Geo. 3 (1772)

21. See Alfred W. Blumrosen & Ruth G. Blumrosen, *Slave Nation* (Naperville, Ill.: Sourcebooks, 2005).

22. United States Constitution, Art. I, Sec. 2, para. 3.

23. *Loving* v. *Virginia*, 388 U.S. 1 (1967).

24. Alexander Keyssar, *The Right to Vote* (New York: Basic Books, 2000), pp. 4, 317, 329.

25. *The Right to Vote*, p. 328.

26. *Citizens United* v. *Federal Election Commission*, 558 U.S. 310 (2010).

27. I criticized this approach and proposed an alternative long before *Citizens United* was decided: "Democracy and Free Speech: A Normative Theory of Society and Government," Chapter 5 of *The First Amendment Reconsidered*, ed. B. F. Chamberlin & C. J. Brown (New York and London: Longman, 1982).

28. That a corporation is a legal "person" has been settled law since the nineteenth century and is not the primary problem. The primary problem is the role of wealth concentrated from any source, including biological persons as well as legal persons.

29. CNN, "There's a sobering truth to Trump's racist tweets that we don't like to admit," July 15, 2019: https://www.cnn.com/2019/07/15/us/trump-tweets-two-americas-blake/index.html

30. *American Prospect*, "America's Civil War," Jine 9, 2020. https://prospect.org/politics/americas-civil-war/

31. Ibid.

32. *District of Columbia* v. *Heller*, 554 U.S. 570 (2008). The dangerous arming of America was a reasonably foreseeable outcome of this decision.

33. *The Nordic Theory of Everything* (New York: HarperCollins, 2016), p. 235.

34. Polls showed that at the time of the invasion, 72% of the U.S. public approved of the war and around 90% felt that the war was going well. Pewresearch.org, "Public Attitudes Toward the War in Iraq: 2003-2008," by Tom Rosentiel, March 19, 2008. https://www.pewresearch.org/2008/03/19/public-attitudes-toward-the-war-in-iraq-20032008/

35. See "Order above the law," *The Economist*, June 6, 2020, pp. 17ff.

36. See "Unseating an old idea" and "What's American for Mitbestimmung," *The Economist*, February 1, 2020, pp. 53-54.

JOHN L. HODGE is a retired health care and public sector lawyer and a former professor of philosophy. He has an A.B. in mathematics from the University of Kansas, a Ph.D. in philosophy from Yale University, and a law degree (J.D.) from the University of California, Berkeley (Berkeley Law). His writings explore the meaning and foundation of democratic society and culture and the impediments of racism, misogyny, and ingrained elitism.

For more information, go to his website at johnlhodge.com and to his blog at johnlhodge.blogspot.com

www.ingramcontent.com/pod-product-compliance
Lightning Source LLC
Chambersburg PA
CBHW021339290326
41933CB00038B/983

9 780983 179092